HOW TO STOP OVERTHINKING IN RELATIONSHIPS

HACKNEY AND JONES

Copyright © 2021 by Hackney And Jones

All rights reserved.

No part of this book may be reproduced in any form or by any electronic or mechanical means, including information storage and retrieval systems, without written permission from the author, except for the use of brief quotations in a book review.

Claim Your Freebie NOW!

Get Good At Problem Solving

Want to know the secret behind getting good at problem solving? Everyone seems to be able to do it, but you're stuck in the pile of endless to-do lists with little progress.

Ok, so how do I get my FREE book?

EASY! See the next page

Claim Your Freebie NOW

Instructions:

1. Open the camera or the QR reader application on your smartphone.
2. Point your camera at the QR code to scan the QR code.
3. A notification will pop-up on screen.
4. Click on the notification to open the website link

Contents

Introduction	ix
1. What Is Overthinking In A Relationship?	1
2. What Is The Side Effect Of Overthinking?	7
3. Why Do I Keep Overthinking In My Relationship?	10
4. Is Overthinking The Same As Jealousy?	12
5. Overthinking And Self-Sabotage	17
6. What Could Be Causing You To Overthink Your Relationships?	20
7. Can Overthinking Ruin A Relationship?	23
8. How Can You Become Aware That You Are Overthinking?	28
9. What Do Professionals Say About Overthinking?	31
10. Famous 'Overthinkers' And Their Experiences	33
11. How Do You Fix Overthinking In A Relationship?	37
12. What A Healthy Relationship Should Look Like	45
13. How You Can Build A Healthy Relationship	52
14. Final Thoughts On Overthinking	56
Feedback	57

Introduction

The word "overthinking" generally comes with a negative connotation. Of course, because in line with Merriam Webster's lexicon, the definition is "Thinking more than necessary regarding something". Judgment of the activity is inherent in its definition. What if we have ceased considering overthinking as a "bad" habit, and began to think about it as a habit that points out something. Individuals labelled as overthinkers are usually regarded as anxious, hyper, ungrounded, or perhaps insecure. All these assumptions might be true, but to be realistic, individuals who think a lot tend to be intelligent, creative, empathic, and like to discover solutions. None of these facets of a person's personality is negative. In fact, they're strengths. It's once these facets of someone's personality go unfed or uncared for that they become "shadow" aspects like anxiety, disorder, ungroundedness, or insecurity. Thinking too often is a habit, very similar to biting our nails. When overthinking becomes problematic is when we frequently overlook the underlying demand behind the behaviour. It's something we begin to do because we're trying to address feelings that might be uncomfortable, or with necessities that aren't met. To be realistic, overthinking won't really fulfil the needs you're trying to deal with. When you continuously ruminate over a certain topic in your mind, there's more likelihood that you won't get anywhere with it. If you're not finding an answer or gaining understanding, then your repetitive thoughts can either produce frustration or can disempower you. Are you still blaming yourself for the error you made last week? Are you still worried about an allergy? Are you still ruminating as regards why your boss isn't responding to your greetings any longer? You're most likely overthinking.

What is overthinking?

Everyone worries from time to time. However, when does worrying become overthinking? Overthinking is solely what its name suggests; thinking excessively. Overthinking is going over exact thoughts over and over again, analysing uncomplicated things or events until all sense of proportion has gone. The overthinking brain cannot translate these thoughts into actions or positive outcomes, thus creating feelings of stress and anxiety. The phrase "overthinking" is often used quite airily of late. As parents, sons or daughters, staff or business folks, worrying about things is connected to caring about our loved ones.

However, individuals who struggle with overthinking tend to be "ruminators", going over events that have already happened. Usually, our worries assist us in moving forward as we are figuring out how to decipher things; however, overthinking tends to be passive rather than being active, dwelling on events that happened in past and establishing disproportionately negative future results. Dwelling on something that has happened in the past and making ruinous predictions are typical examples of what an overthinking mind can do.

Overthinking comes from the primitive emotional part of your brain. Like several traits of hysteria and depression, overthinking actually comes from one of our most primitive instincts. The primitive mind can continuously see things from the worst attainable perspective. This is a result of the fact that the brain is hyper-vigilant, attempting to keep alive. The intellectual brain will tell us that we can't lose our job because we referred to our boss by the incorrect name. However, individuals vulnerable to rumination are responding therein to that primitive fight-or-flight mode, where concentrating on worst-case eventualities is more likely to keep us alive. Overthinking and anxiety work hand in hand, exasperating the feelings of stress and helplessness.

1

What Is Overthinking In A Relationship?

WE SOMETIMES NOTICE ourselves overthinking and overanalysing things from time to time. However, it's usually agreed that nothing positive ever really comes from perpetually overthinking things in a relationship. Relationships are essential for your physical and emotional happiness. Relationships assist in fighting loneliness while also providing you with a sense of purpose in life. Take, for example, the closeness you are feeling with family and friends is an important part of your social support. Relationships in other facets of one's life outside of romance and family can also have a positive result on an individual, like getting along with acquaintances for a shared interest or hobby. Almost all relationships are developed on loyalty, support, and trust. Intimate relationships may also be built on love and affection. Mutual respect and reciprocation of these qualities are vital in maintaining all of your relationships. Otherwise, the relationship might become one-sided.

Overthinking in a relationship can also be related to control. If we're anxious or timid in our ability to keep a positive relationship, we might believe that controlling every facet is the only way to attain a satisfactory relationship. Small negatives (such as holding on for a short while to receive a text reply) become proof of our inability to build a successful relationship, as the mind thinks it has to overwork attempting to get a solution to such a minor issue. To limit overthinking in a relationship, you have to perceive what is and isn't in your control. For instance, many overthinkers in romantic relationships continuously consider and question whether their partner still has feelings for them. You might even find such people saying 'I love you' more frequently, just so they can shortly get confirmation when their partner responds. Understanding how your partner feels about you is most often not in your control. We can only be ourselves, and whether our partner continues to desire us is down to them.

It's quite common for individuals to overthink in relationships, as placing your trust in another individual produces the sort of vulnerability that many find scary and tough to deal with. Despite this, we consistently seek out close relationships, as we are more like social animals and are evolutionarily wired to breed.

Why do I overthink so much?

There are moments you probably wonder why you overthink, and then you are trying to find means to stop overthinking, so it might be counterintuitive for me to suggest that you stop telling yourself that you need to quit "overthinking." Why is that, you inquire? Whenever we enjoin ourselves to stop thinking about something, we straight away start thinking of that very thing. Overthinking is a stealer. It strips individuals of enjoying their loyalty to others because fear refocuses energy and time on what could occur, rather than what is actually happening. The outcome is that one or both parties live in the future, expecting events that may not ever take place.

We overthink because we are despairing creatures trying to find answers. We cherish certainty and control. Never mind, it's a part of human survival tactics. Well, to some extent, overthinking isn't that bad. Probability theory demands that all possible outcomes of an event must be inquired to determine what can actually happen in that given situation. We know what that is like; before an immense event we find ourselves ruminating about it so much, we create conjectural beginnings and endings and even climaxes of the said event before it even occurs. In a way, it is about being ready, so that we can tackle whatever outcome there is and not suffer from a surprising consequence. We can't predict the future, but there is a deep yearning inside of us that wishes we could. Our intuition grants us the ability to do that. This way, we sometimes can perceive when something is not right, where we should or shouldn't go, who we can and can't trust. We possess a powerful inner voice that can sometimes protect our lives. Overthinking tends to put that voice on blast. It is a difficult process to go through but it is sometimes unavoidable.

Overthinking is fear. No one is born with it, it is bestowed upon us either by life experience or traumas that happened to us in the past. Regrettably, we had little or no control over what was taught or done to us during our childhood. Several of us still have roots of fear living inside us since our youthful days. We are victims of this during childhood, friendships, relationships and the gloomy aspect of the experiences latch on to us tightly, the imagination of these past experiences surfaces like a lethal poison oozing through the brain in a single moment of "thinking excessively". We create these destructive thought patterns that are almost inescapable once we start. Stress and emotional fear are not the same. Fear that disrupts our emotions is difficult to categorise as a fear that is assisting us to survive. Hence, all we do is think too much. We succumb to that type of fear and it stresses the brain to the point of irrationality and in some instances, insanity. Additionally, some issues make one overthink. Here are a few:

. . .

ABANDONMENT ISSUES: Abandonment issues involve a deep worry of being hurt, rejected or abandoned. Fear of abandonment is a kind of anxiety that often develops in response to specific painful or traumatic experiences like childhood abuse, neglect, or the loss of a loved one. Abandonment issues are closely connected to insecure attachment styles which are characterised by difficulty building intimate and stable relationships with others. Some people with abandonment issues tend to push people away, remain overly guarded, and avoid being open, while others become needy and mutually dependent.

Abandonment issues come up in an individual's relationships and tend to impact romantic relationships in most cases. Individuals with abandonment issues are more likely to have developed specific defence mechanisms that make it very difficult to build intimate, healthy relationships. The particular types of defence mechanisms an individual with abandonment issues develop varies. These are classified as different "attachment styles." In children, abandonment issues often show up as anxiety, especially when separating them from a caregiver. Kids with abandonment issues may be more easily perturbed and most often have difficulty regulating their emotions. They may display negative attention-seeking traits and have outbursts or tantrums. They can either exhibit avoidant or antisocial characteristics, withdrawing from peers, or bullying others. They might also be either very afraid of adults or overly trusting, developing attributes of dependencies. Adults with abandonment issues will exhibit similar unhealthy patterns in their relationships. Some will push people away, pull away and stop trusting or opening up to people. Others will become excessively needy in relationships and will develop patterns of mutual dependency, relying on the other individual to meet all of their emotional needs. Others with abandonment issues will allow intimacy but become explosive, aggressive, or emotionally reactive with their partner when they feel threatened or disturbed. Each of these distinct patterns represents a specific type of insecure attachment.

ATTACHMENT ISSUES: Normal attachment generally results in feelings of security and trust which forms the base for individuals to explore their environment, build relationships, manage emotions as well as deal with stressful situations. Attachment issues arise mostly in children who have not had a normal connection with a parental figure due to abuse, neglect, institutionalisation or deprivation of care. Children with attachment issues can sometimes experience a developmental delay. They may experience a reduction in academic achievement at school, due to some factors including disruptive traits, withdrawal, and difficulties in relationships with both their peers and authority figures. Signs and symptoms of attachment issues can begin in infancy. However, attachment issues can also progress into adulthood. Adults with attachment issues may be at high risk of developing anxiety, depression and aggressive behaviour. They find it difficult to cope with people in a relationship.

CHILD NEGLECT: Child neglect is a common form of child mistreatment. It tends to affect a child's physical and mental health and can result in long-term consequences such as overthinking. Most adults, parents to be precise, don't understand the depth of neglecting a child. A parent's financial status may also be considered. An impoverished parent, for instance, who finds it difficult to provide children with an adequate meal or shelter, may not be considered neglectful if the family is applying for financial support or if they're doing the best with what they have. Child neglect isn't always the result of a parent failing to attend to their children's needs; sometimes, the options are not available owing to a lack of funds or financial resources. When a child is neglected, this maltreatment affects their overall development and health. Neglect has been connected to eventual physical, psychological, and behavioural consequences. Even if a child is withdrawn from a bad situation, the effect of neglect can last for a long time and can even lead to very risky behaviours and traits like substance misuse and overthinking. Neglect can also lead to attachment issues, self-esteem problems, and difficulty trusting others. Individuals who have been neglected during childhood may struggle to build healthy relationships, and they may experience behaviour disorders or disinhibited social engagement disorder.

2

What Is The Side Effect Of Overthinking?

OVERTHINKING CAN BE SAID to be more than just a nuisance. Science reveals that thinking excessively tolls on one's general well-being. Here are a few side effects of overthinking:

MAY LEAD TO MENTAL ILLNESS:
Are you always attached to your past mistakes? Dwelling on your past mistakes, problems and defects increases the likelihood of being affected by mental health problems. Overthinking can set you up for a vicious cycle that is hard to break. It brings disturbance to your mental peace and as you lose your peace of mind, you tend to overthink.

DISTURBS PROBLEM-SOLVING ABILITY:
Do you sometimes overanalyse things? Overthinkers believe that ruminating over certain situations or problems in the head helps them to overcome them. However, studies claim otherwise. Overanalysing interferes with one's ability to solve problems as it causes you to dwell on the problem and imagine situations that may never happen, rather than finding a solution. Even making simple choices, like selecting an outfit

for the day or deciding on the next holiday spot, may feel like a do or die situation when you are an overthinker. Ironically, all that excessive thinking will never help you make a better choice!

INTERFERES WITH YOUR SLEEP:

If you are a person who overthinks, you probably face problems with sleeping. This is because your body does not allow you to sleep when your mind is not at peace. Ruminating on almost everything and worrying constantly about situations in which you have little or no control often leads to fewer hours of sleep. Hence, overthinking interferes with your quality of sleep and may make you cranky subsequently.

Overthinking can change the way you relate with others and the way you do things. It can significantly affect your personal life, social life and even your life at your workplace. Most importantly, overthinking can also result in emotional distress. To overcome this, you will need to make some changes in your perspective and make a continuous effort to erase away any thoughts that make you feel astray. We, humans, are gifted with intelligence that surpasses that of other beings, and that is what has led us to where we are today, with all of our human inventions: vehicles, houses, electronics, and so on. But what if our brain stops being a utility and starts using us? What if our brain continues to take away our energy by producing unnecessary thoughts and emotions? To comprehend this, we first have to understand what thoughts do. Our thought develops emotions of fear, anger, delight, or excitement. Extremely anxious people are in fact, overthinkers. They create a lot of scenarios on what is going to happen in their brains. It is easy to be overwhelmed with negative emotions like fear, worry, and stress by overthinking a certain matter. Worry about the future hinders one from being in the present moment. Excessive anxiety can make a person miserable and mentally exhausted; hence, one will feel exhausted and sometimes depressed because one's life is being trapped in one's emotions that were created by the person's thoughts. Even worse, anxiety can also result in suicidal ideations and suicide itself. Yes, we can think ourselves to death. Anxiety develops from worrying about the future, and depression comes from worrying about past events. Of course, there might be other causes of depression, like an impairment or a disorder. At its core, depression comes from you thinking about your past repeatedly, which in turn makes you feel very wretched.

3

Why Do I Keep Overthinking In My Relationship?

WHY WE TEND to overthink our relationships is because we feel insecure. This might be from previous relationships where we ended up being traumatised, or because deep down, we don't believe that we deserve happiness. For some of us, immediately when we discover we are in a happy relationship, we fidget and start looking for the most effective way to sabotage it. We believe the person we're relating with will soon discover that they can do better, that we provoke them, or that they're already looking for a reason to leave. This puts us in a defensive position, anticipating trouble, and causes us to seek out problems to mend where there might not even be any.

Yet, we want our partners to assure us, we want them to always be there for us, and we want to know how they feel all the time. But that's not how relationships become a success. People communicate in different love languages, and at times those languages don't sync up. If for instance, your partner doesn't show you the love or affection that you expect, there is a tendency that you might react badly, making assumptions that there is no affection at all. We might then begin to wonder why that is, why can't our partner meet our demands in the way we expect when we require it? From there, we might go on to create problems in the relationship, believing it's already doomed. Of course, none of this is the real scenario, but because of our excessive thinking, we've made ourselves wretched and possibly destroyed our relationship. The more we overthink our relationships, the more likely we are going to notice a fault with them, or to create problems and difficulties that weren't even there. This puts strain on the relationship, which in turn reduces our overall delight in the relationship.

Obsessing over something will never make you feel relieved; it will only leave you with a worse feeling. Our relationships can have a significant effect on our mental health, so it's worth examining how we add to our difficulties when we're struggling with them, and what we can do to make things better for ourselves. When you overthink your relationship, you tend to invite a problem where there isn't one. You concentrate on one segment of your relationship and look search unnecessarily until you find something to get provoked about. This isn't a profitable use of your time and energy, it doesn't make you delighted, and you don't have to carry on doing it. In some cases, it's worth thinking of things in terms of what you can and can't control. You can't control what your partner says, does, or thinks. You just have to accept this. Trying to assume everything they say will leave you mentally drained, and trying to control them might send them away. You can, however, control what you say, do, and think. If you find yourself ruminating excessively, you can stop yourself from going over the edge. Concentrate on how you feel, and then work towards feeling better. Don't let your overthinking have control over your deeds.

4

Is Overthinking The Same As Jealousy?

JEALOUSY IS DEFINED as an intense feeling of insecurity about a potential loss of a privilege or inequity in the distribution of resources. The term is also used to explain a feeling connected with being possessive of another person, such as a partner or friend. Most people experience jealousy continuously, but extreme jealousy can greatly disrupt daily life. People who notice that jealousy interferes with their life may have to consider talking with a therapist to better find out and understand what is causing this emotion.

Jealousy is usually used interchangeably with envy, but the two are entirely different emotions, and each word has a different definition although with similar attributes. While jealousy can be classified as a fear that another person may take something that is yours or something you believe to be yours, envy is the desire for something belonging to someone else. Nevertheless, both jealousy and envy can lead to feelings of insecurity. Envy is more likely to cause feelings of unhappiness and a desire to change. Meanwhile, jealousy is more likely to arouse anger and hard feelings. In some cases, jealousy and envy occur together. When an individual feels jealous, they are likely to envy the person who is causing them to feel jealous initially. For instance, a lady who wants to buy the same new sports car as her neighbour is probably experiencing envy, not jealousy. But a young man whose childhood friend is spending all her time with her new husband, on the other hand, may experience both jealousy and envy. There is a tendency for him to be envious of their relationship and want a significant other of his own, but he might also be jealous of his friend's new marital bond, resenting the reduction in the amount of time they now spend together.

If an individual is jealous, they might indicate it in a wide variety of ways. While some jealous traits are subtle, unclear, or mild, intense feelings of jealousy can cause individuals to act out or hurt others. Signs you may be experiencing jealousy include:

- Provocation toward a person or circumstance that is disrupting something you care about.
- Resentment of a buddy or partner when they cannot give you any attention and spend time with you.
- Difficulty in feeling happy for a colleague when they get something you also want.
- Feelings of hatred toward a new person in a loved one's life are difficult to explain. For instance, a father might have feelings of unfriendliness that result from jealousy toward his daughter's fiance even if the partner that she's chosen is a responsible and healthy choice.
- Deep sorrow or feelings of distance when thinking about a friend, partner or loved one.

IT IS EXPECTED to feel some jealousy, but it can be very helpful to have assistance when working through intense feelings of jealousy, especially if these are grounded in deeper feelings related to self-esteem, trust, or control. Jealousy is a common feeling, and it's experienced by individuals from most cultures. As it can crop up in various situations, jealousy can come in various forms. Some types of jealousy include:

JEALOUSY IN RELATIONSHIPS:

This type of jealousy occurs due to the fear of being replaced by someone else in a cherished relationship. A woman who is annoyed that her husband is flirting with another woman, a husband who feels insecure when his wife spends time with friends, and a teenager who is vexed at her sister for going to the supermarket with her best friend all fall into this category. Jealousy in friendships is often referred to as platonic jealousy, while jealousy in romantic relationships is often called romantic jealousy.

JEALOUSY RELATED to power and social class:

This type of jealousy occurs more frequently in the workplace, as it often relates to competition. For example, an individual who is bitter against their co-worker for being promoted before they were may experience this type of jealousy.

ABNORMAL JEALOUSY:

This is also referred to as pathological jealousy or extreme jealousy, this may be a sign of an inherent mental health issue, such as dementia praecox, anxiety, or control issues. It is often used to explain jealousy that causes an individual in a relationship to have insensible worries about a partner's loyalty in the relationship and may cause them to act offensively or unsafely toward that partner.

It is normal to experience moderate jealousy in a platonic or romantic relationship, and this is not always regarded as being unhealthy. It can show that one cares about the success of their relationship. Nonetheless, jealousy can become disastrous when it is constant, strong, or irrational. A person experiencing a high level of sexual jealousy may have an issue trusting their partner and may check the partner's mail and mobile phone or discreetly follow them. If the partner finds out about this trait, the relationship might collapse. Individuals can become jealous for many reasons. Often, jealous feelings occur as a result of communication issues, low self-esteem, loneliness and differing interpersonal boundaries.

RIVALRY BETWEEN SIBLINGS:

Siblings may exhibit the feeling of jealousy and envy when another sibling is seen as getting more affection, attention, or resources from parents, caretakers or guidance than themselves.

THE FEELING OF INSECURITY:

If one person in a romantic or platonic relationship cherishes the relationship yet feels unsteady in it, they may start to feel jealous. In the workplace, for instance, individuals who feel that their position is looking vulnerable may also feel jealous due to insecurity.

COMPETITION AND RIVALRY:

Vehement competition between pals, siblings, or co-workers may lead to feelings of jealousy if the risks concerned with losing is very high.

DISPOSITION OF PERFECTIONISM:

Individuals with perfectionistic attributes may find themselves feeling jealous if they frequently make comparisons with others about themselves. While these comparisons can also lead to envy, jealousy can also occur when the person with a perfectionist mentality fears that the success of another person will negatively impinge on their success.

HAVING TRUST ISSUES:

Trouble trusting others in relationships may make individuals more prone to feel jealous when their friend or partner spends a lot of time with other people or on their own.

Individuals in polyamorous relationships may also go through jealousy, although not all do. The principal difference between jealousy in a monogamous relationship and a polyamorous relationship is that when jealousy comes about in a polyamorous relationship, it may only involve the individuals in that relationship. It may also involve individuals who are not in the relationship, which is how jealousy happens in most monogamous relationships. A monogamous couple trying out polyamory may also have feelings of jealousy.

In teenagers, jealousy has been connected with both hostility and low self-esteem. Teenagers who sense their friendships to be endangered by their peers also seem to have reduced self-worth and report more desolation than those who do not feel endangered. Girls seem to go through jealousy more frequently than boys do, according to a Developmental Psychology study. A reason for this could be that, as the research shows, girls often anticipate more faithfulness and empathy from their friends. When jealous feelings are existing for a long time, pervasive, or severe, it may show that the cause is an inherent mental health issue. Some mental health problems and symptoms connected with jealousy include dementia praecox, paranoia, psychosis, abandonment issues, anxiety and overthinking. Thus, we can infer that jealousy can result in overthinking.

5

Overthinking And Self-Sabotage

SELF-SABOTAGE CAN BE REFERRED to as when individuals actively or passively take steps to prevent themselves from reaching their goals. This behaviour can have an impact on nearly every facet of life be it a relationship, a career goal, or even a personal goal such as weight loss. Although quite common, it is an implausibly frustrating cycle that reduces a person's self-confidence and leaves them feeling stuck. There are a lot of reasons why an individual may choose to self-sabotage but many stem from because they don't believe in themselves. Psychology nowadays gives a good perception into why and how we self-sabotage. Substance abuse, turning to food, or deferring an action can all be ways in which we self-sabotage. We may also self-sabotage by not devoting ourselves to relationships or being a poor friend even when an association is what we truly want. I've narrowed down what causes this self-destructive trait and what I think are the concrete issues as regards overthinking and self-sabotage.

WE DON'T HAVE SELF-WORTH:
When we do not have confidence in ourselves we can't accomplish our goals. Included in self-confidence is our self-

worth. If we regularly tell ourselves that we are intelligent enough, qualified enough, or smart enough to have what we want, we will act by what we are telling ourselves. The way we talk to ourselves matters a lot and directly have an impact on how we present ourselves to the people around us. When we lack confidence, we tend to do things to hinder ourselves from reaching our fullest potential.

WE ARE AFRAID OF SUCCESS:
When we have worked very diligently for something our success can at times become a stressor. This often occurs when we don't have self-confidence. We may worry that we indeed aren't qualified or ready and that we will be exposed as a deceptive person. Our fear of success makes us engage in doing things that restrict our success. When we are getting very close to reaching a goal we may begin doing things that hinder us from reaching the goal. A business coach can assist if you are afraid of success in your career.

WE PREFER to place fault elsewhere:
When we assume that we are not going to do well or will not succeed no matter what, we start to behave in a way that ensures we will not succeed. When we ruminate over things like "I won't get the job anyway" we displace our commitment towards attaining our goals. When we do fail, because we already told ourselves we would not succeed, the fault can be shifted to someone else. We can justify deferring an action or not getting prepared as we've already accepted that we will fail.

WE DESIRE TO CONTROL:
We feel satisfied when we feel like we are in control. By accepting a pessimistic result ahead of time, we feel like we

are in control even though it is not what we want to happen. We control our failure when we make use of this self-sabotaging thought pattern.

WE ARE AFRAID OF FAILURE:
We are scared that we will give all we have towards ambition and still not be enough. It is easier to give oneself reasons as to why one did not succeed than to truly give it one's all and yet fail. This seems to be the most overwhelming reason why we self-sabotage.

6

What Could Be Causing You To Overthink Your Relationships?

INDIVIDUALS TEND to overthink in relationships owing to fear of rejection, so they start overthinking what the other individual is going to do, say, or feel about them. It's unsettling and redoubtable. You start to look at every activity under a microscope, and not only is it time-consuming and draining, but it could do actual harm to the relationship if you let those thoughts take control, so it's essential to keep things in perspective. When you are about to start a relationship, you need to do the work on yourself, and try to find out why there was an expiry date on your last relationship. Try to identify the problem. Were you too proud, clingy, or needy? Whatever the problem might be, if you are sure that it was an issue in your previous relationship, take the time to go through it, so that it does not appear suddenly this time around. Overthinking occurs when you feel insecure; so make yourself reassured by casting out any old bad behaviours.

Eliminating your feelings with a person you feel comfortable or intimate with, whether it's a buddy, family member, or even a medical doctor, can have a significant impact. They can assist you in gaining a clear perspective on things, and find out if your feelings are real or if you are truly overthinking them. When feelings are involved, our assumptions can often get nebulous, so having an impartial third party is helpful. Another tip is to try and talk it out. It's okay to be vulnerable. Talk about how you are feeling to your significant other. Every healthy relationship has a feeling of security. You should always ask yourself, is it my fear of rejection that is making me think excessively and feel this way? Or is it the behaviour of the individual I am relating with that is making me feel this way? If it is the second one, then you will need to find out if it's a relationship that is worth chasing. It's a potential indication of danger if the other individual has an attribute that makes you second guess every action of yours. To have a successful relationship, we must draw away from our minds. This implies that we must relinquish, surrender, trust and allow the heart to have a prominent position. Individuals in all facets of their lives suffer from excessive thinking. This is like spending time in an inappropriate house, the wrong room and the wrong location. Generally, overthinking is connected with anxiety or worry. It's normal and expected to be thinking about your relationship, but it's essential to be aware of the amount of time you're spending thinking about it. If that is all you ruminate about, that's not right. And if you're spending the majority of your time ruminating about what could happen, or what something might have meant, or what you should have done, then I think it is time to induce some changes.

It is important not to chase people; the right people will show up and stay in your life. It is not possible to be perfect in a relationship. Much better to assume we all tend to make errors, therefore just apologise when you think you have done wrong. Growing up was a process of transiting into adults. Not only physiologically but also mentally. We learned to be accountable, to pay the bills, to complete things and we learned the intricate world of adulthood. To become adults we had to lose our bad tempers, absurdity and our childhood. And we misplaced our minds. The mind of a child is the greatest gift we will ever obtain. In the first ten years of life, our young brain will have stimulated billions and billions of links. It is a supercharged engine for the acquisition of knowledge and creativity. Still, by adulthood, we have thrown away most of this creativity. We now reason like adults. That is why we think excessively and why our thoughts are extremely affected by our knowledge.

7

Can Overthinking Ruin A Relationship?

WHILE OVERTHINKING CAN in some cases be advantageous in some parts of your life when it comes to love and affection, it can be quite detrimental and it can ruin your relationship more than you can envisage. I am not trying to say you should just let loose and not ruminate about anything but ceaseless worrying will bring you nothing but a headache. Sometimes, things can get more complex if you tend to ruminate over every little thing. This holds for difficulties in your relationship as well as ataraxis. Well, the reality is that overthinking only does more harm than good to your relationship. Thinking through a lot is awesome when you are trying to decipher a journey plan. Or concentrating on how to finish an assignment. These issues need thinking through all the obstacles and detour routes. The same can't be opined for relationships though. Overthinking can ruin a relationship. A relationship becomes more difficult for someone who thinks excessively because all your possible scenarios end in you being abandoned by people, them cheating on you or making plans to stab you while you are asleep.

The consequence of overthinking takes into account all the probable paths, even though a bit improbable, and however you might think you are being sensible, you are only losing your repose. Feeling insecure and not conveying it appropriately might bring in a lot of unnecessary mental rumination. But more often than not, overthinking can also occur when you have had previous experiences where you did not give enough attention to a situation. Maybe you have been cheated on and it was only afterwards that you found out that all the signs were right in front of your eyes. So in your relationships subsequently, you no longer have the ability to take words at their face value. You believe that if a man says you are beautiful, he is only doing it to make you feel better or appreciated. Or if your partner admires someone else, you might think you are no longer attractive to them. When you're in a relationship, especially if it is fresh and inciting pleasure, it's comfortable to just drift through the day with thoughts of your significant other in your head. Even as the relationship matures and develops steadily, thoughts reoccurring around your coupledom are well-grounded. Nonetheless, when those thoughts become bigger than you and start to deprive you of your time more and more when you should be concentrating on other important things, it's maybe a good idea to pull on the reins a little. When you begin to obsess over slight things said and unsaid, done or not done, the mind can deceive you into conceptualising things that are not there. Here are ten ways overthinking ruins your relationship:

1. Your hunch destroys the relationship

Since pessimism seems to be your best friend at the moment, positive things seldom get your attention. So an individual whom you are familiar with for quite some time now unexpectedly becomes a likely cheater and an unfaithful person in your head. Even if they do their absolute best and leave no room for you to be doubtful, you can't help but incessantly assume the worst and you even feel they are continuously telling lies in the relationship. Your baseless hunch becomes unbearable for your partner who in the end might want a way out from the relationship.

2. You lose yourself totally while you are overthinking

With all the excessive thinking, you are rarely the same individual anymore. You might hostilely oppose your partner about things, or have emotional blowups about stuff you think is going on. After a few months, you have become a constantly worried, sorrowful individual who picks up fights about unnecessary and minor things. The person you have turned to worries you so well but you are not able to stop being that. You then lose yourself in the process of overthinking.

3. Everything seems to be on the uttermost of the spectrum

Nothing at all has a middle ground. No typical explanation works for you. They just have to be on the uttermost ends of the reason spectrum. As we have earlier said, the way you excessively think takes you to extreme imagination levels.

4. You are incessantly paranoid

The fact that you don't trust people coupled with overthinking makes you grow paranoid. Obsessive-compulsive traits of trying to find out where your partner is every minute of the day are you being paranoid. You even keep ruminating, "Is he really cheating or am I just imagining it?" You aren't able to control your feelings and you keep vanishing into the dark hollow of thinking too much. You also keep thinking of accidents, terminal diseases, fire outbreaks or catastrophes affecting your family. You assume your paranoia is keeping them safe but you are damaging them beyond control.

. . .

5. No resolution, more complexity

Since no rational reasoning is good enough, because you will constantly find a way around it, you surface with eccentric explanations to explicate the reason given. You don't have any solution to your problems and challenges; just an immense pile of more reasonless problems and challenges. Living with you becomes a terrifying thing and you fail to find out that overthinking is ruining your relationship. The incessant stress you feel, you then transfer it to your family. You amplify the difficulties and never think of finding a solution.

6. Trust is no longer in the relationship

While thinking about stuff and also being a pessimist, trust is gone from the relationship. Paranoia might result in a face-off which might cause more of a communication gap. Overthinking mostly occurs when trust can no longer be found in a relationship. If you have a reason to believe your partner is not to be trusted anymore, getting deprived of your peace of mind will not assist anyone. In the process of all this negative thinking, re-thinking and overthinking, trust issues can continue to damage the relationship. Communication is essential in a relationship. It is the key to successful relationships.

7. You tend to build up anxiety issues

Overthinking usually leads to anxiety issues. You are constantly nervous and you develop attributes such as double texting. You get extremely troubled when your partner or your children don't respond to your text instantly and owing to your nature you start thinking the worst, creating a negative scenario in your head. This is how overthinking destroys your relationship. Your partner feels you are ceaselessly after them and monitoring their whereabouts. Hence, you develop anxiety issues.

. . .

8. Your incommunicative overthinking is acting as a silent killer

When you are thinking excessively you might not talk about it always but your actions start working like a slow poison or a silent killer on the relationship. Overthinking can make you a controlling and manipulative individual because you want everything to be according to the way you want it. If it doesn't go the way you want it to you become extremely nervous. So you try your absolute best to keep every circumstance under your control and that makes your partner completely confined.

9. It withdraws all the happiness from the relationship

When last did you spend a whole day with your partner without having a feeling that something bad might happen or a problem might occur? Overthinking in relationships can destroy them because you are never in a happy frame of mind. You keep ruminating about how to make your husband or wife happy but you end up being so tense and nervous that happiness then becomes an illusion in your relationship. Consequently, you feel wretched.

10. Your partner begins to find a way out

Your overthinking becomes such a big problem in your relationship that your partner feels that they now have to look for a way to get out of the relationship. Can you picture how your partner's life is with someone, who is incessantly insecure, nervous, and amplifies every little situation to the worst scenario possible - and keeps complaining about it? It is unavoidable your partner will look for a way out from such a relationship. Once they are gone you will now notice how overthinking has ruined your relationship.

8

How Can You Become Aware That You Are Overthinking?

RUMINATING ABOUT ALL the things you could have done differently, attempting to predict every decision you make, and picturing all the worst-case scenarios in life can be very exhausting. But overthinking is a difficult habit to quit. You might even convince yourself that ruminating about something for a long time is the key to creating the best solution, but that's normally not the case. As a matter of fact, the longer you think about something, the less time and energy you might have to take profitable action. Of course, we all overthink sometimes. Maybe you keep ruminating about all the things that could go wrong when you give a presentation tomorrow. Maybe you've wasted countless hours trying to decide what to wear to that job interview and as a result, you didn't spend any time preparing your answers. Before you can put an end to overthinking, you have to recognise when you're doing it. Here's how to know when you're overthinking.

- **You're not concentrating on solution**

OVERTHINKING IS NOT the same as problem-solving. Overthinking is more about dwelling unnecessarily on the problem, while problem-solving involves trying to find a solution. Imagine that it is about to rain. Here's the difference between overthinking and problem-solving:

OVERTHINKING: "I wish that it will not rain. It's looking like it is going to rain heavily. I hope the house doesn't get damaged because some parts of the roof are already leaking. Why do these things always have to happen to me now? I haven't repaired the roof because my loan hasn't been approved yet. I can't handle this!"

PROBLEM-SOLVING: "I will go and move my belongings away from the apartment with the leaking roof. I'll put will put a bowl out to catch the water droplets from the leak to prevent the rug from being damaged. If we get a lot of rain I'll go to the store to buy some tea so I can cope with the cold afterwards."

PROBLEM-SOLVING CAN RESULT in fruitful or profitable action. Overthinking, on the other hand, incite miserable emotions and does not look for solutions.

- **You experience continual thoughts**

RUMINATING or rehashing the same things over and over again isn't helpful. But, when you're overthinking, you might find yourself replaying a conversation in your head continually or picturing something bad occurring many times. Dwelling on your challenges, errors, and shortcomings, increases your risk of mental health problems, according to a study carried out in 2013 and published in the Journal of Abnormal Psychology. As your mental health diminishes, there is a likelihood for you to ruminate on your thoughts. It's a repetitive cycle that can be tough to breach.

- **Your worrying makes you unable to have a sound sleep**

When you're thinking excessively you might have a feeling that your brain won't close off. When you try to sleep, you might even feel like your brain is on overdrive as it plays back scenarios in your head and makes you picture bad things occurring. Research confirms that rumination interferes with sleep. Overthinking makes it harder to fall asleep. Overthinking impairs the quality of your sleep too. So it's harder to fall into a deep slumber when your brain is busy overthinking everything. Difficulty falling asleep may contribute to more worrisome thoughts. For example, when you don't fall asleep right away, you might imagine that you'll be overtired the following day. That may cause you to feel anxious which may make it even harder to fall asleep.

- **You find it difficult to make decisions**

You might try to convince yourself that thinking for a long period helps you. After all, you're looking at a problem from every possible angle. But, overanalysing and obsessing becomes a barrier. Research shows thinking too much makes it tough to be decisive. If you're indecisive about everything from what to eat for breakfast to which school you should attend, you might be overthinking things. There is a great likelihood that you are wasting a lot of time looking for second opinions and weighing up your options when ultimately, those little choices might not matter so much.

9

What Do Professionals Say About Overthinking?

WHILE SOME PROFESSIONALS are against overthinking, others think that it is what we need. There are worrisome questions that make people overthink: How do we identify ourselves? How do we identify others? How do we identify the societies; small or bigger around us? How do others define themselves? How do others identify us? Simply put, who/what am I? These are the cardinal questions that mankind has been dealing with for thousands of years, and they seem to be unending because of their two contrasting traits. On the one hand, "who/what am I?" is the simplest/easiest question, everyone has an instant answer to it. On the other hand, it might be the hardest question in life because it depends on how identity is conceived. If identity is taken as an absolute structure and as a static trait passed down from ancestors, then the response comes very fast. Nonetheless, if identity is changing rather than static, as a fundamental interaction with life, as being constantly incomplete, non-fixed, the answer gets more complex. What then is identity? Who/what am I? I, like many others, are seeking definite answers to these questions. Curiosity and thirst for answers can be such a great obsession leading to overthinking. Professionals have opined that curiosity and thirst as such tend to make us overthink.

A study was conducted in China as regards overthinking. After the Covid-19 pandemic outbreak in China, many international students were stuck there due to lockdown or quarantine. Their friends and family members were infected by the coronavirus and some died; which affected mental health by worrying and ruminative thoughts. The study explores the impact of rumination and worries on the mental health of a purposively selected group of 300 international students (i.e., Asia, Europe, America, and Africa) in China. Rumination, worry, and the mental health of students were measured by the Rumination response scale, Penn State Worry Questionnaire, and Warwick Mental Wellbeing Scale respectively. The findings of the study revealed that not only rumination and worry had significant negative relationships with mental health but also were significant predictors for mental health. Furthermore, the findings of the study revealed that females had more worries with ruminative thoughts during the Covid-19 pandemic outbreak. Hence, from this case study, we can deduce that overthinking can be very detrimental to the mental health of an individual.

10

Famous 'Overthinkers' And Their Experiences

SOME OF THE greatest overthinkers of all time are Thomas Edison, Orville Wright, Leonardo DaVinci, Isaac Newton and Albert Einstein. Thomas Edison is the inventor of motion pictures, the phonograph and the light bulb – a true genius and great overthinker. Due to overthinking, Thomas Edison had an idea for a car that runs on water but then he thought there already was a car that runs on gasoline and maybe the ideas were too similar. Regardless, Edison felt hydropower would be more affordable for the masses. As an overthinker, studies have shown that Thomas Edison made numerous attempts before his breakthrough came when he invented the light bulb. Edison did not believe in giving up, he believed that it is in overthinking that questions are answered and that life demands rumination.

Issac Newton, the mind behind the law of gravity, has also been considered as one of history's greatest overthinkers. He was psychoneurotic and dedicated to his work. Newton was a rip-snorting experimenter, and the stories of his work and discoveries created while isolated at Woolsthorpe throughout the plague years are popular and well-documented. This is when he developed the binomial theorem that resulted in the discovery of calculus; "He completed his early work on the idea of gravity, and conducted many optical studies; while he also included his work with sunlight. He established this by sending the Sun's light through a slit in a window shade and then passing the light through a prism, he broke the beam into a rainbow. Then, passing the sunshine through a second prism, he found out that the prism was not making the colours, but that they were a property of the Sun's light". Newton also allowed himself to be used as a guinea pig in what might have been a rather unwise attempt to better comprehend colour and vision. During the first half of the seventeenth century, the French thinker René Descartes had projected a nervous idea as regards colour. He prompted that colour perception was caused by pressure exerted on the eye by swirling vortices. Newton examined this and didn't agree.

Newton turned on or argued with nearly everybody within the scientific community of the time. Most popular were his efforts to prove his discovery of calculus. The German mathematician Gottfried Leibniz revealed his work on calculus in the year 1684. Newton instantly tried to prove his precedence and began a resentful argument that lasted for several years. He was also against Huygens, as well as the first Astronomer Royal, John Flamsteed, and several others. He even charged Pepys, his friend, with saying bad things to him. It appears that Newton couldn't stand to be upstaged or picked apart by anyone, friend or contenders. Genius is psychoneurotic, and Newton was no exception. Two of his greatest involvements were religion and the dark art of alchemy. His early list of "sins" clearly shows the depths of his spiritual convictions. One of the Church of England's core beliefs is the doctrine of the Holy Trinity, which opine that God is three separate entities. This doctrine nearly spelt catastrophe for Newton and his career.

In the arena of scientific accomplishment and the pursuit to discover genius, Albert Einstein stands alone. He remains a great essential figure who undertook exceptional, groundbreaking work that not only shaped the pillars of modern physics but to a large extent influenced the philosophy of science. In a literal approach, Einstein transformed the way we see and travel across the world and cosmos. He was the one behind the world's most popular equation and for detecting the theory of relativity, considered to be mankind's highest intellectual findings. Einstein went about his work in distinct ways. From daydreaming to conceptualisation - and even a dash of musical arousal - Einstein's creative insights and philosophical vantage points assist in guiding the work we tackle nowadays. Einstein took a recess from his work to play the violin. Beethoven favoured "long, vigorous walks" in which he made use of a pencil and blank sheet music. Mahler, Satie, and Tchaikovsky all believed in the effect of the constant-scheduled mid-day walk. For some, it's walks and breaks during the day. For others, it's making use of time to a deep interest in areas that are different from their professional field. From music to painting, the pursuance of creative endeavours can assist us in finding and connecting what we know to what we aspire to know. He saw taking music breaks as an important part of his creative process. In addition to music, he was an advocate of 'combinatory play' taking seemingly unrelated things outside the core of science (art, ideas, music, thoughts), and syncing them together to come up with new theories. This was how he came up with his most popular equation, $E=mc^2$. As a fifteen-year-old, he dropped out of high school. Einstein left school because his teachers didn't approve of visual imagination for learning, skills which became cardinal to his way of thinking and perception. "Imagination is more essential than knowledge," Einstein would say. It's no coincidence that around the same time, Einstein started to use thought experiments that would change the way he would think about his perspective experiments. His first, at age sixteen, saw him pursuing a light beam that would help establish his discovery of special relativity. His innate ability to conceptualise and operationalise complicated scientific details became a hallmark of his research. His work on gravity was influenced by picturing riding a free-falling elevator. This flight of fancy finally led him to comprehend that gravity and acceleration were essentially the same. Using these simple thought experiments, Einstein was able to realise that time and space are both shaped by matter; the basis for the idea of general relativity. Amazingly, this thought experiment changed everything we thought we knew about the world. Newton's ideas of the world were one-dimensional, but Einstein suggested that our universe was four dimensions, where stars, planets, and celestial bodies formed a "fabric" that were dynamically influenced by the synchronising and curving of gravitational pull. Only recently has humankind been equipped to dig into much of what his theory had proposed; supernovas, black holes, and the evolution of our solar system.

Nearly a century later, Einstein's bequest remains solid as ever. His ideas of gravity, space, and time continue to influence a new generation of scientists. As Einstein proceeded with his work, he maintained a natural sense of comprehension of the world and compassion and kindness about people around him. It's only fitting that he was very cognisant of the unbelievably short time we have on this universe, while at the same time comprehending that all the work he achieved was directly related to those who came before him. It's cheering to know that he found out that his work would be helpful for all those who had yet to arrive. "How strange is the lot of us mortals! Each of us is here for a short journey; for what purpose he knows not, though he sometimes thinks he perceives it. "But without in-depth reflection, one knows from daily life that one exists for other individuals a hundred times daily I remind myself that my inner and outer life are based on the labours of other men, living and dead and that I must put myself to use to give in the same measure as I have received and am still receiving," Einstein said.

11

How Do You Fix Overthinking In A Relationship?

MEETING someone that you hope to be with for a very long time is so exciting. It can also be nerve-racking, especially if you get in your head or become excessively obsessed about it. Once you start thinking excessively in a relationship, it can feel like you're holding up a magnifying glass in an attempt to find and stop inherent problems so that everything turns out very fine. But experts have opined that overthinking in such a way does more damage than good. We all tend to overthink. The key is trying to differentiate when it's a once in a while happening from when it's becoming a serious issue, one that can destroy even the strongest relationship. If you are continuously obsessing over "what if" scenarios, then basing your actions on events that have not even occurred, consider it a sign overthinking has gotten out of hand and that you can no longer control it. The same is true if it seems like you're never living in the moment, but instead ruminating about the past or worrying about what the future holds. When that is the case, you are no longer concentrating on your relationship, which is one reason why overthinking in a relationship has the tendency to separate you and your partner. Bearing that in mind, here are effective ways to fix overthinking in your relationship:

. . .

1. Try sending texts and move on

Should I say "heey," "what's up" or "hello"? I want to seem casual. Should I wait five minutes to text back? Or 15? While it can happen to anyone, agonising over what to text a person is most common in the early days of a relationship. It's normal to be excited and anxious about a new potential relationship however overthinking can also lead to its destruction. Not to mention, if you say "hi" instead of "heey" and it results in a breakup or separation, they were not someone you needed to be with anyway. So try to relax, send the text, and move on with your day. Allowing yourself to balance your life and this new individual will help you not overthink it.

2. Do not reread their texts

While there are times when it's very necessary to read into an individual's text and craft the perfect response like if you're arguing, everyday texts don't need a reread. So if you catch yourself combing through them or looking for an issue, stop! If a certain text is bothering you, call the person to talk, instead of trying to "figure out" how they feel by overthinking.

3. Avoid overanalysing their body language

The same is true in person, where you might catch yourself looking for signs of trouble in a person's intonation or body language. If that's the case, you might be overthinking your relationship because you have unclear communication. The person might be speaking in generalities and that can leave you wondering what they specifically meant. To find clarity, work on improving your communication with each other. That way you won't have to invent answers because you'll already have them.

. . .

4. Enjoy and appreciate the present phase of your relationship

Instead of always thinking about what the future holds and the end goal of the relationship, take time to enjoy whatever phase you're in currently. It is good to predict what might happen in the future, but obsessing excessively about the future can become a problem. Realistically, we all have no control over our future. We all just strive and hope for the best. If ruminating about the future has become a deeply ingrained habit, it might take some time to correct. But keep correcting yourself and soon you'll be more concentrated on what is going on around you instead of what may or may not happen down the road. Be grateful for the journey so far and exhibit an optimistic mindset.

5. Stay grounded and focused

Overthinkers often struggle to trust that what they see and experience is the entire truth. It's why they have underlying anxiety and sometimes ponder whether someone likes them, or whether the relationship will work out or not. Staying focused helps keep your mind clear of unrealistic scenarios that you sometimes just picture in your mind. Grounding helps you stay in the present and will reduce the anxiety and tendency to allow your thoughts to spin unnecessarily. So remind yourself to live in the present rather than dwelling on the possibility of negative outcomes. Erase every pessimistic mindset and assure yourself that the relationship is moving in the right direction.

6. Challenge and criticise your assumptions

Overthinking about the likelihood of cheating or other toxic situations is so easy to do and you might be vulnerable to such excessive thinking. But keep in mind obsessing over "what if" scenarios rarely prevents them from happening.

The anxiety and lack of trust tend to drive couples apart. When you're anxious and overthinking, you're not in the moment, so you're not able to truly enjoy time with the person and if you're not present, how can you possibly develop in your relationship? The next time a person doesn't text back right away, flip the script from "Oh, he/she's probably ignoring me" to "I'm sure he's just busy with work." This process will begin reprogramming your brain so you stop assuming the worst.

7. Concentrate on personal accomplishment and fulfilment

Individuals can certainly do things to make you feel insecure or unsure about your relationship. But if all is well and you still feel unstable, consider taking that overthinking energy and reinvesting it in yourself. Find ways to remain fulfilled, possibly by hanging out with other people, starting a hobby, taking a class; working towards feeling good about your own life as an individual. If you start to feel comfortable with yourself, you won't be as daunted by normal ups and downs in your relationship. Focus on the goals and ambitions you have accomplished. Think about a pleasing memory or a holiday. When you try to deviate the mind a bit from the relationship issue bothering you, you tend to mitigate overthinking. Your mind wanders off a bit from anxiety and worries and then you feel relaxed.

8. Work on believing in your intuition

If you get an intense feeling that something is not right, don't over-analyse it. Instead, trust that your intuition is trying to tell you something regarding it, and do something about it right away. In doing so, you'll spare yourself the helix and you'll also make your instincts to be sharper in the future. Rather than questioning or doubting your intuition, why don't you believe your intuition for once? Give no room for pessimism!

9. Ask for advice only when it is needed. Make it less often

Our friends and family members are great people to turn to for outside perspectives, relationship advice, etc. But if you rely on others to assist you in making every single relationship decision, you'll end up with too many opinions, making it easy to overthink. Allow yourself to take a break from requesting external advice. Instead, use that time to relax and evaluate how you feel. As time goes on, you'll learn to trust your own opinion and judgment of a situation. Do not always depend on suggestions and others gives you concerning your relationship. Be aware that not everyone wants your progress. Some people want your downfall and others might be jealous of your relationship. Hence, seek external advice less often.

10. Base your beliefs on concrete evidence

Try to always base your thoughts on evidence rather than made-up facts. We get ourselves very worked up by picturing what other people are doing or saying or thinking about us. Instead of doing this, please challenge yourself to only believe things you can find actual or concrete evidence for. Worried an individual is mad at you? Go find evidence. If there's no (or little) evidence, assume you are not the problem and that he/she's probably upset about something else.

11. Don't take everything personally

While this is way easier said than done, practise not to be taking things personally. Is someone in a bad mood? Fine! It's not a reflection on you as an individual, and it certainly doesn't mean they care about you any less. They might probably be worried about something else. Do not just jump to the conclusion that it has something to do with you or the relationship.

12. Know that you will be just fine

Overthinking takes place when you want to prevent a negative outcome. But if you remind yourself things will work out regardless, it can provide big relief. Connect to the idea that you will be alright no matter what happens and suddenly the panicked overthinking will calm down. Believe that everything is under control and there is no issue at all. Erase that negative perception. Be optimistic!

13. Adjust your goal

If you kick back and decide to wait for the truth to be revealed instead of making it your personal goal to obsess and overthink you will take a large burden off yourself. Be patient. Try holding on and not conceptualising any scenario in your head. Let your thought process be based on reality and not what you think, feel or perceive. This you can prevent overthinking.

14. Communicate and be open

Let's assume you overthink because you are worried your relationship with an individual isn't going anywhere. Instead of fortune-telling also known as making assumptions, why don't you just ask? Talk to the person about your fears or concerns. By opening this line of communication, you can discuss in detail how your relationship is going now, and also make plans for the future. That way you'll both remain on the same page, and no unnecessary assumptions will be required.

15. Stay busy and occupied

The moment you start overthinking, try to make yourself busy. Call a friend, go for a walk, do that project you've been putting off. If you're accomplishing something, you won't have time to overthink. When you are occupied with an activity or a project, the tendency for you to overthink is very low. Being idle might make you overthink. Hence, get busy or socialise.

16. Update yourself about psychology

Are you overthinking throughout the day? Try reading more about cognitive distortions, such as overgeneralisation, mind-reading, magnification, personalisation and hysteria. Knowledge is power, and understanding why your mind is captivating you can help reel it back in. When you are informed, there is a tendency for you to utilise the information

17. Take a deep breath

You can also get out of your head and into the moment by making using mindfulness skills such as taking deep breaths, counting all the items around you that are blue, or even playing a favourite song and singing every lyric. These tricks help bring you back to reality, so you aren't hyper-focused on scenarios like "what ifs."

18. Place your focus on something positive

If you feel your mind running away from reality, stop and think about something positive. It helps to have a few things queued up ahead of time. Make a list of topics that you like to think about and focus on that topic. Think about your best memories, a holiday, your pet, a great vacation you went on. Just make sure it isn't related to something you're ruminating about like your relationship.

• • •

19. Try reconnecting with your values
When we're caught up in our thoughts, we're often disconnected, distrustful, or avoidant. So instead of letting that vibe take over, refocus on the kind of person you want to be. Get in touch with important values, like compassion, assertiveness, and authenticity. Think about how you might act if those scary thoughts never showed up and try acting on your values instead of your thoughts.

20. Visit a therapist
If the habit of overthinking has become truly overwhelming, consider talking to a therapist. The tendency to overthink may be a sign you were hurt in a past relationship, and are now on high alert due to lingering fear and anxiety. It can take time to work through deeply ingrained relationship trauma and to break these types of habits but if it results in learning how to stop overthinking, the effort will be worth it.

12

What A Healthy Relationship Should Look Like

HEALTHY RELATIONSHIPS INVOLVE SINCERITY, trust, respect and open communication between people and they take effort and compromise from both people. People who respect each other's independence, can make their own decisions without fear of retribution or retaliation, and share decisions. If or when a relationship ends, there is no stalking or refusal to let the other person go. But just as important is learning to identify when a relationship is going well. A lot of people are unsure of what to look for, or worse yet, they are not aware of all the positives that they truly deserve to have within a relationship. If an individual grew up watching their parents or other family members act out chronically toxic patterns, then that person may very well come to define those patterns as "normal" and thus finding it difficult to understand the baseline of what a good relationship looks like. Bearing that in mind, here is a place to start. Healthy, functional relationships have the following and they shouldn't be optional:

1. Communication

Communicating with honesty and respect, especially about very difficult things, is something that does not come automatically to everyone. We may have learned to keep discomforting things under the surface for the sake of harmony or the appearance of perfection, or we also may have never even learned how to accept difficult feelings to ourselves. Other problems and challenges involve escalating a conflict into an intense quarrel: lacking the ability to not take things overpersonally or lashing out when we feel endangered. It is alright if you have these tendencies; what's important is that you work on them, as strong and healthy communication is the lifeblood that develops good relationships.

2. Trust

Trust is arguably among one of the most important relationship characteristics. Without trust, there is a lack of a concrete foundation on which to build emotional closeness, and your potential for hurt over and over again grows ever bigger. Without trust, you will be left ceaselessly unsure of whether you can count on the individual to come through for you, and whether or not they are honest and mean what they are saying. There are many ways to build and rebuild trust in a relationship, but if you are not on the path to doing so, your relationship is quite vulnerable to stress, anxiety and uncertainty.

3. Empathy

Being willing to take another person's perspective or view can be helpful in so many cases whether in parenting, being a good neighbour, or even just letting someone merge in front of you on the highway. But it is arguably most essential with the person you've chosen as a friend, partner or playmate. Can you truly put forth the effort to try to comprehend their view, even when you disagree with it? Does their pain incite you to try to help them feel better? Do you feel delighted when you triumph? Empathy is essential for a long-term relationship.

4. Patience

No one can be perfectly patient every time, and factors such as lack of sleep, stress, or physical health problems will make one more easily agitated at various points in one's life. That's part of being human. But people in a healthy, loving relationship extend each other a basic common denominator of patience that allows gives room for peace, flexibility, and support when one person is having a bad day or is not at their best. When people are chronically impatient with each other, they often develop a dynamic of bean-counting and resentment, where they are mentally racking up the offences that the other individual has committed. Being able to adjust to the ebb and flow of a person's mood in day to day life within reason can instead allow a feeling of being unconditionally loved.

5. Affection and Interest

Affection should be an aspect of any healthy and committed relationship. More subtle than love is the expression of that love in the form of affection and also a genuine interest and liking of each other. Small physical gestures of affection, like hugs, kisses, and comforting touch, can go a long way to keeping each person feeling loved, comforted and secure within their relationship. There is no one right amount of physical affection within a relationship as long as both people feel comfortable with how their needs match up. The same is true of physical intimacy. As for the "like" factor, this goes further than love and affection, it means that you are truly interested in each other and fond of each other and that you are together out of attraction (even if you no longer have the physical infatuation of the early days) rather than obligation.

6. Flexibility

Relationships take compromise. And while some things don't allow for a perfect scenario, the key component that makes for good compromise is important no matter what: flexibility. Both individuals must show flexibility in day-to-day life and decision-making because if it is just one person always doing the bending, that imbalance can grow toxic over time. In healthy relationships, both people are willing and ready to adjust as needed to the changes and growth (positive and negative) that may come about during a long-term relationship. And they can evaluate on a joint level, especially during conflicts and misunderstandings, what matters most to each person within the relationship, and how that should be prioritised. Two people who are never willing to bend to meet the need of the other will be on separate paths altogether before long a far cry from truly having a long-lasting relationship.

7. Appreciation

The research about the importance of gratitude and appreciation within relationships is striking; it makes us feel happier and more secure with our people. And the more that we feel that gratitude, the more we feel appreciated for who we are within relationships, which also develops the relationship's well-being. Even little expressions of gratitude and appreciation can help improve relationship satisfaction. So the next time you think it doesn't matter whether you say "thank you" for something a person did, think again. And maybe consider the negative feelings we all tend to have when we notice a lack of appreciation over time.

. . .

8. Room for Growth

Relationships grow stale not just because a certain amount of time has elapsed, but because people feel stuck and unable to move forward, either as individuals or as a couple. It is unrealistic and downright unhealthy to expect that two people will remain the same across months, years, and decades of a relationship. Hopes, fears, goals, and interests constantly evolve, and that is a very good thing. A relationship doesn't have to end or even suffer because of this, as long as both people allow each other the space to grow, by not pigeonholing each other into their younger selves, by trying to take an interest in learning what's important to the other person, and by not setting inflexible expectations.

9. Respect

We often associate the concept of respect with people or concepts that are not intimate with each other: respecting one's elders, respecting symbols of religious faith, or respecting authority. But respect is every bit as important in a relationship, if not more so. In healthy relationships, people talk to each other in ways that don't debase, invalidate, or belittle. They value each other's time and opinions like they value their own. They protect each other's privacy and don't use each other as the butt of jokes or as hired help to constantly clean up the apartment or make a thankless dinner. When respect begins to erode within a relationship, it is a long and painstaking road to build it back. The damage is far easier to do than undo.

10. Reciprocity

In healthy relationships, the tallying that early relationships show ("She picked me up at the train station last week, so I owe her a favour") fades into the background as a new, trusting equilibrium takes its place. You both just generally do for each other when needed. In an ideal situation, the give-and-take roughly works out to equal over time, and neither person feels resentful. Of course, in many relationships, the give-and-take won't ever become equal. For example, one person needing long-term medical care, one who is naturally a more happily nurturing person, or one who struggles with a psychological disorder. And that can be okay, as long as both people feel comfortable overall with the level of give-and-take as it exists, and they each find a way to give something to the relationship especially in the form of emotional support when they can.

11. Healthy Conflict Resolution

Much research has pointed to the fact that the way people argue or don't can predict a lot about their relationship's success. We are willing to entertain conflict in the beginning, but once people ride off into the sunset together, we expect that things should be okay from then on out. Ironically, people that hide their upset with one another to preserve the illusion of everything being perfect are probably far worse off than the people that express their emotions and work to resolve them as they come up, even when it causes conflict. In short, healthy relationships refrain from stonewalling and escalating into personal attacks when there is a difference of opinion or a problem. They can talk it through with respect, empathy, and understanding.

12. Individuality and Boundaries

Two people who were the same would probably not have much to talk about after a while; after all, they'd already know what the other's perspective would be, so why bother to listen to it? Of course, two people who are so different that they don't share each other's values or daily styles of living are bound to have too little in common to maintain an interest in each other (at best), or be downright incompatible, disliking each other from the start (at worst). The sweet spot is a relationship where the similarities create a foundation to connect, but individual differences are still respected and valued. Moreover, each person must be given the freedom to still live their own life, especially in terms of friendships, professional goals, and hobbies. A strong, healthy relationship brings to mind a Venn diagram. There is adequate overlap to keep the connection strong, but each person has aspects of their lives that are theirs alone, and that boundary is respected by both parties.

13. Openness and Honesty

Different people have different levels of openness within their relationships. Some might be horrified at leaving the bathroom door open, for instance, whereas others will discuss the most intimate of physical details with each other without giving it a second thought. So too is the case with openness about hopes, dreams, and even the details of one's workday. But no matter where you fall on the spectrum of letting it all hang out, it's important that there is a solid match and that honesty underlies whatever disclosures you do make. People who mask their true selves, hide their emotional realities or actively deceive other people about their habits and behaviours are jeopardising the fundamental foundation of trust that every relationship needs.

13

How You Can Build A Healthy Relationship

HEALTHY RELATIONSHIPS WITH YOUR PARTNER, friends and family members can enhance your life and make everyone feel good about themselves. They don't just happen though; healthy relationships take time to build and need work to keep them healthy. The more positive effort you put into a relationship, the healthier it should be. People in healthy relationships love and support each other. They help each other practically as well as emotionally. They are there for each other in the good times and the bad times. Lack of respect, trust, open communication, equality both shared and individual interests, understanding, honesty and care are signs that a relationship is not healthy. People who have healthy relationships are more likely to feel happier and satisfied with their lives. They are less likely to have physical and mental health problems. One of the most profound experiences we can have in our lives is the association we have with other human beings. Healthy and supportive relationships will help us to feel healthier, happier, and more satisfied with our lives. So here are a few tips to help you to build a healthy relationship in all areas of your life:

1. Acknowledge and celebrate differences

One of the biggest challenges we experience in relationships is that we all differ. We can perceive the world in many ways. Certainly, a stumbling block that we come across when we try to build relationships is a desire or an expectation that people will think as we do and, in this way, it is so much easier to create a rapport. We feel more comfortable when we feel that people understand us and can see our point of view. Life, however, would be very dull if we were all the same and, while we may find it initially easier, the novelty of sameness soon would wear off. So accepting and celebrating that we are all different is a great starting point in building a healthy relationship.

2. Give people your time and attention

Giving time to people is also a huge gift. In a world where time is of the essence and we are trying to fit in more than one lifetime, we don't always have the time to give to our loved ones, friends, and work colleagues. Technology has somewhat eroded our ability to build real rapport and we attempt to multi-task by texting and talking at the same time. Being present in the time you give to people is also important, so that, when you are with someone, you are truly with someone and not dwelling in the past or worrying about the future. The connection we make with other people is the very touchstone of our existence, and devoting time, energy, and effort to developing and building relationships is one of the most valuable life skills.

3. Listen effectively

Listening is a crucial skill in boosting another person's self-esteem, the silent form of flattery that makes people feel supported and valued. Listening and understanding what others communicate to us is the most important part of successful interaction and vice versa. Active or reflective listening is the single most useful and important listening skill. Inactive listening, we also are genuinely interested in understanding what the other person is thinking, feeling, wanting, or what the message means, and we are active in checking out our understanding before we respond with our new message. We restate or paraphrase our understanding of their message and reflect it to the sender for verification. This verification or feedback process is what distinguishes active listening and makes it effective.

4. Develop your communication skills

Communication occurs when someone understands you, not just when you speak. One of the biggest dangers with communication is that we can work on the assumption that the other person has understood the message we are trying to get across. Poor communication in the workplace can lead to a culture of backstabbing and blame, which, in turn, can affect our stress levels, especially when we don't understand something or feel we have been misled. It also can have a positive effect on morale when it works well and motivates individuals to want to come into work and do a great job.

5. Manage mobile technology

By now, pretty much everyone has a mobile phone and many people have two or more. While they are a lifesaver in an emergency and an effective tool for communication, they also can be a complete distraction when people exhibit a lack of mobile phone etiquette.

6. Learn to give and take feedback

Feedback, in my opinion, is the food of progress, and while it may not always taste great, it can be very good for you. The ability to provide constructive feedback to others helps them to tap into their potential and can help to forge positive and mutually beneficial relationships. From your perspective, any feedback you receive is free information and you can choose whether you want to take it onboard or not. It can help you to tap into your blind spot and get a different perspective.

7. Learn to trust more

Trust is very essential in a relationship. Studies have ascertained that trust is hugely important in any relationship. "To trust is more important than love." I believe that sentiment is true because no love will last without equal amounts of respect and trust.

8. Develop empathy

There is a great expression that I learned a long time ago: "People will forget what you said, people will forget what you did, but people will *never* forget how you made them feel." Empathy and understanding build connections between people. It is a state of perceiving and relating to another person's feelings and needs without blaming, giving advice or trying to fix the situation. Empathy also means "reading" another person's inner state and interpreting it in a way that will help the other person and offer support and develop mutual trust.

EVERY RELATIONSHIP we have can teach us something, and by building healthy relationships with others, we will be happier and more fulfilled and feel more supported, supportive, and connected. Ensure that the relationship you have is a healthy one.

14

Final Thoughts On Overthinking

IN CONCLUSION, one important thing I suggest you do when you're overthinking is to name it. Simply acknowledging that you're overthinking, feeling anxious or worried, can help interrupt the cycle. And this acknowledgement is also your cue to try some of the other strategies. Write down your worries. If you're stuck in an overthinking loop, I recommend writing down your worries. Putting them down on paper creates a "holding place" for them so you don't have to keep them all in your head and then seek therapy. If your overthinking overlap common sense or inherent reactions, you probably should see a therapist. Overthinking situations is a common problem for most people and I believe it has something to do with our survival instincts. However, if it becomes socially and psychologically debilitating, it could be an underlying symptom of an anxiety disorder, which should be addressed and treated by a qualified medical professional. You might also want to get a journal and habit tracker to see your progress and pattern as you seek therapy. Additionally, focus on yourself, work on yourself and set goals that are not attached to anyone.

Feedback

Thank you for reading 'How To Stop Overthinking in Relationships'. We hope you enjoyed the book? If you have a free moment, please leave us some feedback on Amazon.

Also, scan the QR code below to visit our website where you can find more information on our range of books available.

 HackneyandJones.com

www.ingramcontent.com/pod-product-compliance
Lightning Source LLC
Chambersburg PA
CBHW031546080526
44588CB00018B/2719